Table of Contents

Low-Cost Balkan Recipes for You!

Taste The Balkan Peninsula with Less Than $50!

BY: Ida Smith

License Notes

Introduction

This cookbook is a beautiful collection of low-cost Balkan recipes that you can enjoy right there in your home!

With this under $50 Balkan cookbook, you have cut costs in many ways.

First, you don't have to travel to the Balkan Peninsula to enjoy the Balkan cuisines.

Second, you don't have to go over your budget to prepare the cuisines.

Either way, you get to enjoy delicious Balkan meals and drinks without spending too much!!!

Koktel Cufte

These meatballs are exceptionally delicious!!

Prep time: 05 minutes

Cooking time: 2 hours

Servings: 2

Ingredients

- 1 lb. meatballs
- 8 oz chili sauce
- 4 oz grape jelly

Directions

Combine the grape jelly and chili sauce in a cooker.

Cook till the jelly dissolves.

Add the meatballs.
Cook till done.

Saganaki

Cheese never looked or tasted this hot!!!

Prep time: 04 minutes

Cooking time: 08 minutes

Servings: 1

Ingredients

- 100 g thick Monterey jack cheese slice
- 1 tablespoon lemon juice
- 1 cup olive oil
- 40 g flour

Directions

Wet the cheese slice.

Coat with the flour.
Fry the coated cheese in a pan of the oil.
Garnish with the lemon juice.

Turos Csusza

This cheese and egg pasta delicacy is a major culinary turn on!!!

Prep time: 08 minutes

Cooking time: 10 minutes

Servings: 2

Ingredients

- 1 dash salt
- 1 smoked bacon slice
- 3 oz cottage cheese
- 4 oz egg pasta
- 8 tablespoons sour cream

Directions

Preheat the oven to 352 degrees F.
Cook the egg pasta al dente.
In a skillet, cook the bacon slice till crisp.
Crumble after draining.
Put the pasta in a baking dish.
Add the sour cream and salt.
Spread the cheese all over the pasta and sour cream.
Bake for 4 minutes.
Serve the pasta with the bacon slice.

Rakija

No, you don't want to miss out on this Balkan's brandy!!!

Prep time: 09 minutes

Cooking time: nil

Servings: 1

Ingredients

- 14 tablespoons lemon lime soda
- 2 oz pomegranate juice
- 2 oz Rakia liquor
- 1 sliced small lemon
- 2 mint leaves
- Ice cubes

Directions
Add ice to a glass.
Add the Rakia liquor.
Add the pomegranate juice and soda.
Stir well.
Add the lemon.
Add the mint leaves.
Stir well.

Dunav Fisherman's Stew

All you desire in a fish stew!!!

Prep time: 20 minutes

Cooking time: 10 minutes

Servings: 2

Ingredients

- 1 bay leaf
- 2 cups cooked mixed river fish
- 1 chopped yellow onion
- 40 ml sunflower oil
- 2 peppercorns
- 1 diced medium carrot
- 1 minced garlic clove

- 40 ml chopped celery root
- 1 cup fish stock
- 1 tablespoon pepper
- 1 teaspoon salt
- 2 cups mashed tomatoes
- 1 handful chopped parsley
- 2 basil leaves
- 1 dash thyme
- 40 ml tomatoes juice
- 1 dash anise seed
- 1 teaspoon red wine vinegar
- 1 dash cayenne pepper
- 1 teaspoon hot paprika powder
- 1 teaspoon sweet red paprika powder

Directions

Sauté the bay leaf and peppercorns in a pot of the oil.
Cook for 1 minute.
Add the celery root, onion and carrot.
Cook for 3 minutes.
Add some water. Cook till the veggies become mash.
Add the paprika powders and garlic.
Cook for 3 minutes.
Add the fish stock and mashed tomatoes.
Add the fish, herbs, pepper, salt, spices and tomato juice.
Cook for 6 minutes.
Add the vinegar.
Cook till the vapor of the mixture is sticky against your palm.

Topla Cokolada

This creamy hot chocolate is all you need to keep warm in winter!!!

Prep time: 05 minutes

Cooking time: 10 minutes

Servings: 2

Ingredients

- 2 oz chopped semi-sweet chocolate
- 350 ml cold milk
- 1 teaspoon vanilla sugar
- 60 g granulated sugar
- 2 oz chopped dark chocolate
- 2 g cornstarch

Directions

Combine 280ml of the milk and the sugars in a pot.

Cook till it boils. Turn off the heat.
Add the chocolates.
Mix well to melt the chocolates.
Turn on the heat.
Combine the remaining milk and the cornstarch in a bowl. Mix well.
Stir in the cornstarch mixture into the chocolate-milk mixture.
Stir everything till it thickens.
Serve immediately.

Bambus

Cola + Red wine!!!!

Prep time: 05 minutes

Cooking time: nil

Servings: 1

Ingredients

- 8 tablespoons Pepsi
- 70 ml red wine

Directions

Combine both in a glass.

Creamy Garlic Mint Feta Sauce

Either with salmon, beef, chicken or turkey, this creamy Balkan sauce can take our $50 any day!!

Prep time: 07 minutes

Cooking time: nil

Servings: 6

Ingredients

- 1 teaspoon salt
- 1 minced garlic clove
- 3 tablespoons feta cheese
- 8 tablespoons Greek yogurt
- 1 tablespoon lemon juice
- 1 tablespoon chopped mint
- 1 teaspoon chopped dill

- 1 teaspoon water

Directions

Combine the garlic and 1 pinch of the salt to form a paste.
Add the remaining ingredients.
Mix well.

Smreka

This drink is not only delicious but healthy too!!!

Prep time: 04 minutes

Cooking time: nil

Servings: 1

Ingredients

- 1 cup water
- 2 handfuls dried juniper berries
- 1 tablespoon lemon juice
- 1 teaspoon coconut sugar
- Ice cubes
- Mint leaves for garnishing

Directions

Combine the sugar and berries in a jar of the water.
Add the lemon juice.
Keep aside for 9 days.
Strain into a glass of ice.
Garnish with mint leaves.

Goulash

This Balkan pasta and beef combo is – exhilarating!!

Prep time: 10 minutes

Cooking time: 20 minutes

Servings: 3

Ingredients

- 1 minced garlic clove
- 1 teaspoon canola oil
- 1 diced medium green bell pepper
- 1 handful diced onion
- 1 lb. ground beef
- 1 cup beef broth
- 9 oz diced tomatoes

- 9 oz tomato sauce
- 2 teaspoons Worcestershire sauce
- 5 tablespoons shredded cheddar cheese
- 1 teaspoon salt
- 1 bay leaf
- 1 teaspoon Italian seasoning
- 1 cup raw macaroni noodles

Directions

Sauté the onion, beef and bell pepper in a pan of the oil.

Cook till the beef is well cooked.

Add the garlic. Cook for 20 seconds.

Throw in the broth, salt, Worcestershire sauce, tomato sauce, seasoning, tomatoes, macaroni noodles and bay leaf.

Cook till the noodles are soft.

Throw away the bay leaf.

Add the cheese.

Kuletos Shirley Temple

Shall we worship at this temple??!!

Prep time: 04 minutes

Cooking time: nil

Servings: 1

Ingredients

- 25 ml ginger ale soda
- 25 ml lemon soda
- 25 ml lime soda
- 8 ml grenadine
- Ice cubes
- Maraschino cherry for garnishing

Directions

Combine all of the ingredients in a shaker of ice.

Shake well.

Strain into a glass of ice.

Garnish with a maraschino cherry.

Slatko od Dunja

This is an experience of a lifetime!!!!

Prep time: 10 minutes

Cooking time: 1 hour 15 minutes

Servings: 2

Ingredients

- 2 oz chopped walnuts
- 6 oz sugar
- 1 lb. peeled diced quinces
- 5 oz water
- 2 tablespoons lemon juice
- Coffee to serve

Directions

Combine the water, sugar and lemon juice in a pot.

Add the quinces.
Cook and allow simmering for 40 minutes.
Before the quinces get done, try as much as possible to skim off foam.
Serve the quinces syrup with coffee. Garnish with the walnuts.

Vampire Victim

This is the perfect Halloween cocktail!!!

Prep time: 04 minutes

Cooking time: nil

Servings: 1

Ingredients

- 1 medium egg white
- 2 oz scotch
- 1 oz amaretto
- 3 oz cherry brandy
- 1 handful sprinkles
- Ice cubes

Directions

Strain the egg white into a shaker of ice.
Add the remaining ingredients except for the
Shake well.
Wet the tip of your glass with water.
Coat the rim with the sprinkles.
Strain the mixture into the glass.

Monastery

What can we say??!!

Prep time: 07 minutes

Cooking time: nil

Servings: 1

Ingredients

- 2 muddled basil leaves
- 1 dash plum preserves
- 1 oz maraska slivovitz
- 1 dash honey syrup
- 1 dash lemon juice
- Ice cubes
- Peychaud's bitter and basil leaf for garnishing

Directions

Throw the basil leaves in a shaker of ice.
Add the remaining ingredients.
Shake well.
Strain into a glass.
Garnish with Peychaud's bitter and basil leaf.

White Bean Salad

This delicacy is a genius piece of work!!!

Prep time: 05 minutes

Cooking time: nil

Servings: 2

Ingredients

- 1 pinch salt
- 1 tablespoon chopped red onion
- 8 oz white beans
- 1 dash lemon juice
- 1 dash crumbled dry herbs de Provence
- 1 teaspoon pepper
- 1 teaspoon canola oil

- 1 teaspoon white vinegar

Directions

Put the onion and lemon juice in a bowl. Toss well. Keep aside.
Put the remaining ingredients in a bowl.
Add the onion mixture.

Shopska Salad

If you want to find out why this delicacy is the Balkan's national salad, here is one way to find out!!!

Prep time: 10 minutes

Cooking time: nil

Servings: 2

Ingredients

- 1 cup dressing
- 1 tablespoon chopped parsley
- 2 chopped roasted red peppers
- 2 chopped large tomatoes
- 1 chopped medium yellow onion
- 1 chopped medium cucumber
- 3 tablespoons crumbled feta cheese

Directions

Combine all of the ingredients except for the dressing and feta cheese in a bowl.

Toss well.

Add the dressing. Mix well.

Serve and garnish with the feta cheese.

Jellyfish Shot

Wow!!!cs

Prep time: 05 minutes

Cooking time: nil

Servings: 1

Ingredients

- 2 oz chilled white crème de cacao
- 2 oz chilled grenadine
- 2 oz chilled bailey's Irish cream
- 2 oz chilled Disaronno amaretto

Directions

Pour the de cacao into a shot glass.

Layer with the amaretto.

Layer with the bailey's Irish cream.
Add drops of the grenadine to form tentacles.

Kompot

This homemade apple and berry Balkan juice will make you kiss the store bought version goodbye!!!

Prep time: 04 minutes

Cooking time: 06 minutes

Servings: 2

Ingredients

- 100 g chopped mixed fruits (berries, apples, peaches and grapes, etc.)
- 1 cup water
- 15 g granulated sugar

Directions

Boil the water for 2 minutes.

Add the fruits.

Cook for 4 minutes.

Turn off the heat.
Stir in the sugar.
Allow cooling before serving or serve chilled.

Screwdriver

This is definitely not what you are thinking about!!!

Prep time: 06 minutes

Cooking time: nil

Servings: 1

Ingredients

- 2 dashes orange bitters
- 1 dash sugar syrup
- 2 shots vodka
- 2 shots orange juice
- Ice cubes

Directions

Combine all of the ingredients in a glass. Stir well.
Add ice.

Balkan Yogurt

It is time to tick this awesome Balkan yogurt off your yogurt bucket list!!

Prep time: 20 minutes

Cooking time: 10 minutes

SERVINGS: 2 cups

Ingredients

- 5 g yogurt starter
- 1 l whole milk
- 3 tablespoons powered milk
- 8 tablespoons low-fat milk

Directions

Combine all of the different milk types in a pot.

Cook for 10 minutes.
Turn off the heat.
Allow the mixture to sit till the temperature is 110 degrees F.
Then, stir in the starter.
Cover the pot. Wrap up the pot with a large blanket.
Keep in a warm space for 13 hours.
Transfer the mixture into a lined colander.
Put the colander in a bowl.
Wrap up with the blanket again for another 2 hours.
Chill for 3 hours.

Boza

Have you had a cold winter drink before? Bet you haven't!!

Prep time: 20 minutes

Cooking time: 30 minutes

Servings: 1

Ingredients

- 10 tablespoons millet
- 19 tablespoons sugar
- 5 cups water

Directions

Add the millet to a pot.

Add the water.

Cook till soft.

Blitz the mixture till smooth.
Pour into a bowl. Add some sugar. Mix well.
Cover the bowl. Keep aside in a cool place for 3 days.
Make sure that you stir every day.
Strain into a cup.
Chill for 2 days.

Tarator Soup

Perfect for you!!

Prep time: 08 minutes

Cooking time: nil

Servings: 2

Ingredients

- 1 minced garlic clove
- 1 peeled and diced medium English cucumber
- 1 dash salt
- 1 cup water
- 1 tablespoon chopped dill
- 1 tablespoon sunflower oil
- 1 cup Greek yogurt

Directions

Combine the dill, garlic, oil, cucumber and salt in a bowl.

Add the water and yogurt.

Mix well to remove any lumps.

Chill for 20 minutes.

Serbian Coffee

You are in for a real treat!!!

Prep time: 04 minutes

Cooking time: 07 minutes

Servings: 1

Ingredients

- 1 pinch sugar
- 70 ml water
- 1 tablespoon ground coffee powder

Directions

Boil the water.

Add the sugar.

Turn off the heat. Add the coffee.
Stir well.

Brodet

Mouthwatering delicious!!

Prep time: 08 minutes

Cooking time: 40 minutes

Servings: 2

Ingredients

- 3 scampi
- 1 tablespoon pepper
- 1 tablespoon salt
- 6 cleaned de-bearded mussels
- 4 tablespoons chopped tomatoes
- 300 ml water
- 2 medium chopped onions

- 3 minced garlic cloves
- 4 tablespoons chopped parsley
- 2 tablespoons white vinegar
- 30 ml olive oil
- 1 kg mixed fish
- Bread to serve

Directions

Sauté the onions and garlic in a pan of the oil.
Cook for 3 minutes.
Add the water and tomatoes.
Cook for 7 minutes.
Add the fish.
Add more water to cook the fish well.
Add the pepper, salt and vinegar.
Add the scampi one by one.
After 5 minutes, add the parsley and mussels.
Serve with bread.

Cobanac

This recipe will help prepare you to join other contestants in the next 'Pozeski Kotlic" competition!!!

Prep time: 10 minutes

Cooking time: 20 minutes

Servings: 2

Ingredients

- 1 lb. mixed chopped meat (beef, pork, etc.)
- 100 g grated peeled carrot
- 150 g chopped onion
- 1 tablespoon sweet red paprika powder
- 10 g grated parsley root
- 1 tablespoon olive oil
- 1 pinch hot red paprika powder
- 1 l water

- 1 teaspoon salt

Directions

Sauté the onion in a pan of the oil.
Add the parsley root and carrots to the onion.
Cook till it becomes a paste.
Add both paprika powders.
Add the meat. Add the salt and water.
Cook till done.

Riblja Corba

Hold your culinary breath because this fish soup is going to blow your mind!!!

Prep time: 10 minutes

Cooking time: 25 minutes

Servings: 2

Ingredients

- 1 chopped celery stick
- 1 kg scaled mixed boneless gutted fish
- 1 sliced carrot
- 1 tablespoon olive oil
- 1 sliced onion
- 1 minced garlic clove
- 1 tablespoon chopped parsley

- 2 peppercorns
- 8 tablespoons risotto-styled rice
- 1 tablespoon salt
- Bread to serve

Directions

Sauté the onion in a pan of the little oil.

Transfer to a bowl.

In a pot, add the fish, peppercorns, salt, onion and vegetables.

Cook for 20 minutes.

Add the rice and remaining oil.

Serve with bread.

Walnut Martini

Walnuts never tasted any better!!!

Prep time: 06 minutes

Cooking time: nil

Servings: 1

Ingredients

- 1 oz Tuaca liqueur
- 2 shots vodka
- 1 shot dry vermouth
- 1 shot walnut liqueur
- Ice cubes

Directions

Combine all of the ingredients in a shaker of ice.
Shake well.
Strain into a glass.
Enjoy!!!

Cvarci

Just when you think you have tasted pork in all variations of the world, Balkan's Pork Crispy says, "We are just getting started!!!"

Prep time: 08 minutes

Cooking time: 20 minutes

Servings: 2

Ingredients

- 3 g whole onion
- 700 g cubed skinless white bacon

Directions

Put the bacon in a pot.

Cook till the bacon is melted.

When it becomes golden, add the onion.

Fry for 5 more minutes.

Rozata

Nothing prepares you for what is coming to your mouth!!

Prep time: 07 minutes

Cooking time: 25 minutes

Servings: 1

Ingredients

- 1 tablespoon dark rum
- 2 tablespoons sugar
- 4 tablespoons sugar caramel sauce
- 2 eggs
- 150 ml milk
- 1 tablespoon grated lemon zest
- 1 teaspoon vanilla sugar

Directions

Preheat the oven to 301 degrees F.

Dissolve the sugar in a pot of the milk.
When it dissolves, turn off the heat.
Combine the vanilla sugar and eggs in a bowl.
Add the rum and zest.
Add the milk.
Stir well.
Strain the mixture into serving bowls.
Add the caramel sauce to each bowl.
Put the bowls in a deep baking tray of hot water.
Bake for 20 minutes.
Allow cooling for 4 minutes.
Cover the bowls.
Chill well before serving.

Kuletos Martini

Flavorsome!!!

Prep time: 06 minutes

Cooking time: nil

Servings: 1

Ingredients

- 20 ml Bombay Sapphire
- 20 ml vermouth
- 20 ml Grey Goose
- Ice cubes

Directions

Put ice in a shaker.

Add all of the liquids.
Mix well.
Strain into your glass.

Conclusion

Here you have it!

The 30 Balkan recipes that you don't have to stress your pockets to cook. With less than $50 for each, you can prepare the meals seamlessly with either cheap store-bought ingredients or the ones you have at home.

Don't allow money to stop you from enjoying the awesomeness of Balkan traditional recipes; create low-cost culinary Balkan masterpieces with the 30 Balkan recipes in this cookbook.

Don't miss out!

Visit the website below and you can sign up to receive emails whenever Ida Smith publishes a new book. There's no charge and no obligation.

https://books2read.com/r/B-A-LRXL-YDVQB

BOOKS 2 READ

Connecting independent readers to independent writers.

www.ingramcontent.com/pod-product-compliance
Ingram Content Group UK Ltd.
Pitfield, Milton Keynes, MK11 3LW, UK
UKHW061655190726
13853UKWH00008B/2217